Did they Exist ?

Anthony Wootton

Nelson

contents

ROC

Can you imagine a bird so huge that it is able to kill and eat elephants and lay eggs big enough to fill a large room? No, neither can I, although if you read *The Arabian Nights* (also commonly called *The Thousand and One Nights*) you'll find that Sinbad the Sailor tells of encountering such a fantastic creature during one of his ill-fated sea voyages.

It happened, it seems, on his Second Voyage. Sinbad and his crew had sailed out of the Persian port of Basra, down the Red Sea and far out into the Indian Ocean, until eventually they landed on an uninhabited island 'rich in flowers and fruits'. Here, Sinbad becomes separated from his companions and discovers a colossal egg, though he doesn't recognize it as one at first because he describes it as taking fifty paces to walk round!

Eventually, while Sinbad crouches in the vast egg's shadow, the parent bird arrives, so huge that it blots out the sun with its great wings. Ignoring our hero, it settles down to hatch its egg and Sinbad, rather daringly, ties himself to one of the bird's talons (unwinding his turban for the purpose), as a means of getting himself back to civilization when the bird takes to the air again. All goes well and Sinbad is able to escape when the great bird lands on top of a hill, a considerable distance from the original island.

Sinbad apparently knew of the bird's reputation for feeding itself and its young on elephants, so we may wonder how on earth he managed to escape being eaten. Well, we are not told. Perhaps the *roc* — as Sinbad called it — didn't even notice him or felt he was scarcely worth bothering about. After all, to a monster like that, he would scarcely have made a decent mouthful!

Well, it's a lovely story, of course, but nonsense as it stands. Throughout the long history of the world, no bird has ever approached anything like the size of Sinbad's roc. It couldn't, because it would collapse under its own weight. Nor would it be able to fly, even if it had hollow bones, as all flying birds possess to make them lighter. The largest bird known today, the African ostrich, is gnat-sized compared with Sinbad's roc, but has only small wings, quite useless for flight. In fact, the bulkiest birds which are able to fly are bustards and swans, and they are considerably smaller than ostriches.

On the face of it, then, we ought to be able to dismiss Sinbad's account as just a pleasant myth or fairy tale, based only on the story-teller's highly vivid imagination. However, there may be a little more to it than that because, strangely enough, it is possible to piece together some sort of factual back-ground that may explain at least parts of the story, even allowing for exaggeration.

Bustard.

To do this, we need to return to the area of Sinbad's sea trip, which you will recall began where the Red Sea joins the Indian Ocean. If his ship had sailed more or less due south, it might have brought him to a large island called Madagascar (now called the Malagasy Republic) where, strange to tell, huge birds *did* once live. They were nowhere near the size of the fabulous roc, of course, but they were still very large. Sixty centimetres taller than the ostrich, to which they were closely related, they also laid eggs of a truly vast size. These great birds — which, like the ostrich, couldn't fly — have been given the scientific name of *Aepyornis titan*, and are among the largest birds ever to have lived on Earth. They are now extinct but probably only finally disappeared a few hundred years ago, so they would certainly have been living at the time *The Arabian Nights* was written, about 850 A.D.

RED SEA

AFRICA

INDIAN OCEAN

MADAGASCAR

Madagascan rain forest.

Could it be, therefore, that the *Aepyornis* formed the basis of Sinbad's roc, suitably magnified for effect? It seems quite possible because, for many centuries, the civilized world knew very little of Madagascar and any information about the living *Aepyornis* would probably only have reached outsiders in the form of vague, half-understood rumours. No one really *knew*, so they made up stories about it — stories that made the roc vastly bigger than it was and capable of doing impossible things, like flying, feeding on elephants, and laying eggs as big as a shed. It is not surprising, because a tendency to describe things as being much greater than they really are has been part of story-telling throughout the ages. Present-day anglers often do much the same thing when describing the fish that got away from them!

Many islands of the Indian Ocean were once home to large birds, now extinct - the dodo, the solitaire, the moas, the titan - which may well have contributed to the roc legend.

Didus solitarius.

Dodo.

Of course, there are other ways in which tales of the roc might have grown 'taller' in the telling. The *Aepyornis* was almost certainly much hunted by the native Madagascans and it is quite possible that parts of the birds — bones, feathers, or even eggs — were sometimes offered as curiosities to occasional traders from Egypt, Persia and Arabia. Indeed, the famous Venetian explorer Marco Polo (1254—1324) tells of a roc's feather that was sent to Kublai Khan, after the great Mongol emperor had expressed interest in legends of the bird. That, it seems, was probably a forgery, or something else, but think of the effect that an *Aepyornis* egg, or even a piece of one, might have had on someone who had never seen the living bird. The ostrich's egg is big enough, but the *Aepyornis's* eggs are immense — about one metre round, with the capacity of six ostrich eggs or about 150 chickens' eggs! (Since one of these great eggs could hold over four litres, the native Madagascans often used empty ones for storing liquids.) If you take that comparison to its logical conclusion, the *Aepyornis* ought to be *many times* the size of an ostrich, not just sixty centimetres taller (three metres, as compared with two and a half). No wonder exaggeration crept in and made the *Aepyornis-roc* as big as an office-block!

The fascinating and rather sad thing about the *Aepyornis-roc* — or 'elephant-bird', if you like — is that it may well only have become finally extinct in the early part of the nineteenth century. Until then, even scientists had not really believed in it, partly because the island was difficult to explore and inhabited by people hostile to outsiders. When they did finally come to take an interest in the birds, it was too late. The last few remaining individuals had finally been wiped out, by a

The court of Kublai Khan.

Eggs of the Elephant bird, Ostrich, Chicken.

Ostrich egg hatching.

combination of over-hunting and forest clearance, and the only evidence left was bones and eggs perfectly preserved in the island's sands and swamps. Some of the eggs even contained half-formed chicks.

It is strange to think that if modern ideas of conservation had been applied all those years ago, the living basis of Sinbad's fabulous roc might be seen in zoos today!

11

phoenix

In John Masefield's lovely book, *The Box of Delights*, the boy, Kay Harker, is asked by Cole Hawlings, the mysterious Punch and Judy man, which of all the world's birds he would most like to see. Kay thinks for a moment and then replies, 'The *phoenix*'. He hesitates a little before making his choice because he is not sure the bird even exists. Nevertheless, his wish is granted and he sees his phoenix, which just goes to show what a writer's imagination can do, because Kay was right in the first place. The phoenix never really existed, except in people's minds, and if we look at what the old stories tell us about it we can see why.

The idea goes back to Ancient Egypt, where we find the phoenix described as a handsome, eagle-like bird, with part-golden, part-red plumage, that spent most of its life in the Arabian deserts. It was rarely seen and, according to one version of the story, only appeared in Egypt once every five hundred years, when it flew to Heliopolis, 'city of the sun', and deliberately burnt itself to ashes by settling on the altar flame there! However, it seems it did not really die because from those same ashes a young, fully formed phoenix was born and flew away, presumably back to Arabia.

It is pretty obvious from all this that no one has ever seen or will see a living phoenix, except in a dream or as an illustration in a book of myths. The interesting thing is, though, that we can find certain clues which may explain one aspect of the Egyptians' idea. It may sound incredible, but some birds are apparently quite fascinated by flames and small fires, especially members of the crow family, such as rooks, carrion crows, and jays. One zoologist actually proved this by setting fire to some straw near to a tame rook. Far from becoming nervous and backing away, as we might expect, the bird went and deliberately stood over the flames, with raised and vibrating wings. It didn't get burnt, but the image it presented by its strange behaviour was almost exactly like that shown in illustrations of the mythical phoenix!

Just why birds should occasionally behave in this strange way is not clear. One idea is that they carefully use the heat of the flames to relieve the irritation caused by their feather mites, a type of parasite which all birds have. Sparrows probably have a similar idea in mind when they 'bathe' in the smoke issuing from chimney pots. Whatever the reason, it is quite possible that the Ancient Egyptians saw birds behaving in this way, from time to time, and used it as the basis of their phoenix myth, adding fanciful details which closely linked it to their worship of the sun and their belief in resurrection, or life after death.

Nowadays, of course, the phoenix is much less important to us than it was to the Egyptians (who had a whole range of animal-based gods and goddesses), although in one sense the idea of it lingers on. Modern fire insurance companies employ the phoenix as one of their favourite symbols, with the bird being shown with raised wings arising out of a sea of flame. The idea behind the logo is that if your property is destroyed by fire the company will help you to build it up again (always provided, of course, that you insured with them first!). Phoenix, the capital city of the American state of Arizona, also reflects the idea in a slightly different way. When the city was founded in the 1870s, local people discovered that it was being built on the remains of a much more ancient, long-vanished Indian settlement, so they thought it would be nice to suggest that the town had been reborn from its ashes, just like the bird of mythology.

# Dragons

A little to the east of the Indonesian island of Java lies a group of smaller islands which includes Komodo, Rintja, Flores, and Padar. The islands are not widely known, in themselves, but they are famous to zoologists as being the home of a remarkable animal, the largest of all known lizards. These great reptiles are known to scientists as *Varanus komodoensis*, but their popular name is *Komodo dragon*, which is appropriate because they are probably the nearest the world has ever come to the far more fantastic dragons of myth and legend.

St George and the dragon.

17

Komodo dragon.

Of course the Komodo dragon does not have the mythical dragon's wings. Of all reptiles known to have lived on Earth, only the long-vanished *pterodactyls* have ever flown. Nor does it breathe fire. That would be an impossibility. But it *is* large — up to three metres long — and powerful. What is more, it fits the 'dragon image' in being a flesh-eater, capable of killing animals as big as a buffalo, by first severing their leg tendons and bringing them crashing to the ground. It will even attack man if he takes too many liberties!

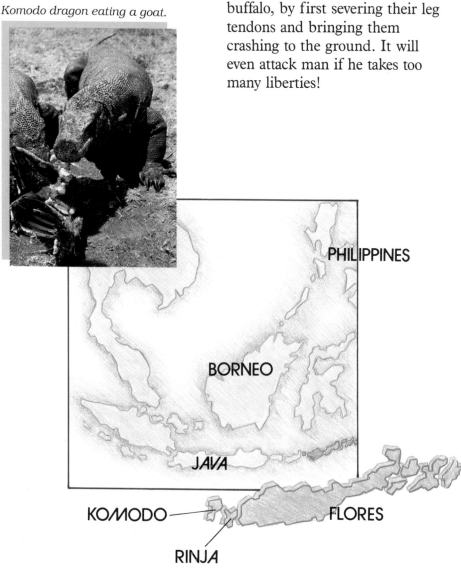

Komodo dragon eating a goat.

PHILIPPINES

BORNEO

JAVA

KOMODO

RINJA

FLORES

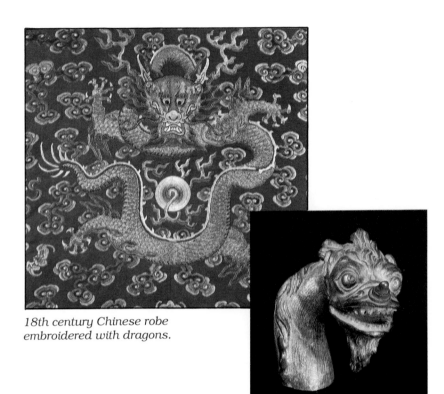

18th century Chinese robe embroidered with dragons.

Dragon emblem of Yang, c.1800.

Perhaps not surprisingly, there are those who believe that the Komodo dragon may have given the Chinese, Japanese, and other Asiatic peoples, the basic idea for their own mythical dragons. What is certain is that the fictional dragons are usually far more weird and dangerous than any living beast. In fact, they came in all shapes and sizes, might live on land or in the sea, and were firmly believed in throughout the world.

Dragons formed a particularly important element of the myths of Europe, but they also occur in traditional tales from Africa, the Middle and Far East, in pre-Columbian America, and even in some of the islands of the Pacific.

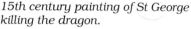
15th century painting of St George killing the dragon.

A typical European or classical (Greek or Roman) dragon might have a long, scaly body ending in a tail which sometimes bore a deadly sting. It also had clawed feet, like those of a lion, a bat's or eagle's wings and a horned head with red, staring eyes. A simpler one was like a huge snake, with or without wings, that wound itself about great hills and crushed its enemies (often human) in its huge coils.

Centuries ago, belief in dragons like these was so strong that tales of them and their encounters with man became extremely common. Any unexplored region was suspected of harbouring dragons and old maps can often be seen with the unknown areas labelled 'Here be dragons'. In Medieval times, so legend tells us, it became almost the duty of noble 'knights errant', or those seeking fame and fortune, to track the beasts to their lairs and kill them. There are many famous tales such as the Greek hero, Perseus, rescuing the beautiful Andromeda from a fire-breathing dragon, and the famous battle between St George (the patron saint of England) and a dragon, said to have taken place in Berkshire, at a place now known as Dragon's Hill.

Needless to say, the majority of these dragons were no more than figments of the storytellers' imagination. However, it is possible that some dragon stories were based on early man's encounters with animals that were strange and new to him and therefore perhaps terrible.

Men of Alexander the Great battling with dragons.

Greek vase painting of Jason regurgitated by the serpent.

Carpet python.

Those dragons described as a snake or 'great worm' are of particular interest because 'dragon' actually derives from the Greek word, *drakon,* for a snake or serpent. Perhaps, then, some of the mythical snake-like dragons have their origins in early sightings of the huge pythons of India and Africa, or even of fights with them, for pythons have been known to attack and even kill man. Pythons overcome their prey by constriction, winding themselves about their victims and choking them to death, just as many dragons were supposed to do. This snake-like appearance may also explain why man felt dragons had to be killed as a matter of course, whether they were threatening or not, because the snake was, in early times, the symbol of evil.

Pythons do not naturally live in Europe so some of the strange 'dragons' described in old English records and traditional tales must have been large snakes, such as cobras, or perhaps crocodiles, brought back from foreign lands. Animals like these would probably have been regarded with terror by simple country people and if someone had been killed or injured by them then that, too, would have helped to spread exaggerated tales of them far and wide.

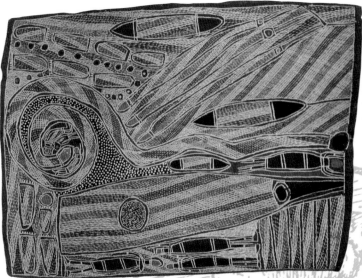

Aborigine bark painting of the Great Python.

Cobras are, of course, deadly poisonous, while crocodiles have a habit of knocking their potential victims down by a sweep of their muscular tail. Both these things add to their dragon image and link to the 'stinging tail' feature mentioned earlier as being typical of many dragons of myth and legend. As such tales spread and were told and retold down the ages, the 'dragons' developed into far more fantastic creatures, with added features like wings and the ability to breath out flames. Needless to say, anyone who managed to kill a 'dragon' would have been hailed a hero!

Dragon lore is thus based on real animals and superstitions brought together in fanciful tales of mythical monsters. Another example of this is their ability to kill just by looking. The classical basilisk was a serpent said to kill with its breath or stare and the cockatrice, part-cock, part-snake, killed with a mere glance. In the past people firmly believed in the 'evil eye', the power of certain animals and men to bewitch with a look. This evil power must have become linked to the reptile's watchful gaze.

Most lizards have a very fixed stare and snakes do not even have eyelids, which might render a look from one of them (especially a large one) particularly blood-chilling and suggest that the reptile ('dragon') was trying to enchant the onlooker — or worse! If you have read Rudyard Kipling's *Jungle Book* you'll recall that the boy, Mowgli, is told never to look the great python, Kaa, directly in the eye, for a similar reason.

Another interesting point which links fiction and fact is that many large reptiles have red, orange, or yellow mouths, with a narrow forked tongue that darts in and out like a flickering flame. Some years ago, when explorers in New Guinea captured a specimen of a monitor lizard, closely related to the Komodo dragon, they showed the animal to a local priest. After looking at the lizard for a moment, the old man pointed to its mouth and said, 'Fire'. When I add that the local name for this rarely seen creature is *'Artrellia'*, or dragon, it is not difficult to understand how belief in fire-breathing dragons arose.

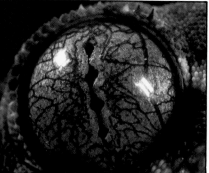

Gecko eye.

Diamondback head.

ea-serpents

Nowadays we know a good deal more about the animals that live on the world's land surface than our ancestors did. Creatures, unknown to us in olden times and once regarded as monsters, are now accepted, named, and neatly classified. New animals may turn up in the future but they are, on the whole, unlikely to be large.

The seas, however, are a very different matter because we are not a great deal better equipped to explore them than our ancestors were. For a start, there is the sheer size of the task. Over seventy per cent of the world's surface is covered in sea and some parts of it are as much as ten kilometres deep — far deeper than Mount Everest, the world's highest mountain, is high. Then there are the practical difficulties of exploration: the problems of breathing underwater for any length of time, and the tremendous pressure exerted by the water at great depths. Even to see properly underwater for more than a few yards is difficult because there is very little light so far beneath the surface. It is all very frustrating for scientists investigating marine life because, from what little we know, it is clear that a great variety of life can live in the depths of the ocean and survive pressures that would squash a man flat in no time at all!

These physical facts make it likely that there are still a great many quite large, perhaps very large, animals living in the world's oceans that are unknown to science. It is less easy to scoff at those many tales of great sea monsters — 'sea-serpents' — which have been told by sailors and explorers from ancient times right up to the present day. The problem is getting to know what they really are

Humpback whale.

Capture of a giant squid (6 metres long) by the French gunboat, Alecton, in 1861.

because they are nearly always extremely elusive and descriptions of them vary so much.

Many sea-serpents observed in the past may, of course, simply have been animals that were unfamiliar to the observer or seemed somehow different at a distance, such as whales or giant squid, but others are difficult to link with any known animal.

The commonest type of sea-serpent
— the one most frequently described right
down the centuries — is said to be like a
huge snake, varying in length from about
seven metres to over thirty metres. As the
serpent moved through the water its body
showed as humps above the surface. It was said
to have a horse-like or whiskered cat-like head,
with eyes of varying size and, sometimes, small horns.
The head generally protruded out of the water at an
angle, held on a long neck, and sometimes a kind of fin
or mane ran down the middle of the creature's back.
Others have been described as being like huge
crocodiles, twenty metres long, while still more are said
to have the appearance of vast turtles or even giant one-
eyed tadpoles!

*Dutch ship attacked
by a giant fish.*

Horrible monsters of the northern seas, by Sebastian Munster, 'Cosmographia Universalis', 1544.

However, it is virtually impossible to say just what these creatures are because they cannot be definitely linked to known animals and none of them has ever been captured, or washed up on the seashore. One thing we can say is that they are unlikely to be snakes — even though 'snake' is really just another name for 'serpent'. A giant snake would certainly not fit the descriptions of those sea-serpents that are said to move in vertically undulating coils because no snake (or fish or eel, come to that) could possibly progress in that way. Whether on land or in the sea, snakes can only move by sideways coilings.

Olive sea snakes.

The curious thing is that there *are* sea-snakes in some parts of the world, although they have little in common with the sea-serpent of myth and legend. For one thing, they do not grow beyond a length of about three metres, have quite thin bodies, and are only found on the surface of tropical seas, whereas sea-serpents are generally reported to be much larger and have been observed in almost every part of the world's oceans. Further, no true sea-snake coils its body when it swims, as the mysterious sea-serpent is supposed to do.

Some people trying to identify these reported sea-serpents suggest that they may really be a unusually large kind of leopard seal, so far unknown to science. Known species of leopard seals live mainly in the southern seas, particularly about the Antarctic Circle, but cryptozoologists (students of unknown animals) think it is possible there may be others with a much wider range. It is certainly true that existing leopard seals display features that fit some of the sea-serpent descriptions. They are not very large (up to about three metres), but that in itself is not a disqualification because it is often very easy to exaggerate the size of animals seen from a distance. In any case, we may be talking of a much larger, unknown kind of leopard seal!

The seals certainly swim rather in the way that the fabled sea-serpent is said to do — by alternate forward plunges and surfacings, rather like a human being doing the butterfly stroke, only far more gracefully. The leopard seal also commonly pokes its large whiskered head out of the water and may show one or two humps, formed by its back and tail, as it swims. The only problem with linking leopard seals with sea-serpents is that we really ought to see them far more often and so be able to identify them, because seals are mammals and no mammal can exist for long at great depths.

Leopard seal.

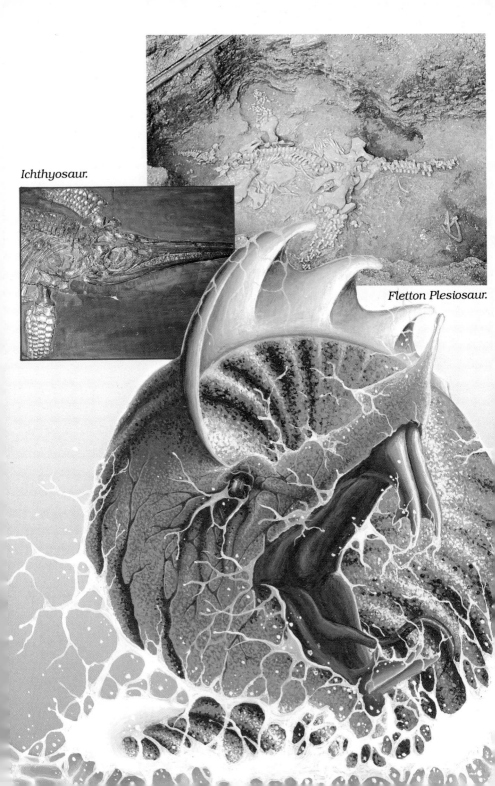

Ichthyosaur.

Fletton Plesiosaur.

Other students of strange, unidentified animals suggest that at least some of the sea-serpents reported from around the world could be a species of unknown whale, of a type called *Basiliosaurus*. These whales are only definitely known to us today from fossils but some feel that their descendants may still exist in certain areas. If so, they would fit many sea-serpent descriptions, because fossils show that these great mammals attained a length of some twenty-two metres, with a tapering body and large tooth-filled head.

Some people suggest that the answer to the sea-serpent mystery lies in the survival of extinct marine dinosaurs, such as the ichthyosaur or plesiosaur. There are those who say that the famous Loch Ness Monster could be a plesiosaur, too.

Still more ideas include the possibility that sea-serpents are really giant marine worms or that they could be a dense cluster of backboneless creatures called *tunicates* which cling together in great numbers. Tunicates are really quite small in themselves but, as larvae, form one vast rather snake-like community sometimes about thirty metres long and thirty centimetres across. They even move in the way that the classical sea-serpent is alleged to!

Of course, all these suggestions are not very much more than guesswork. As I have said, no one really knows what sea-serpents are: they may be unknown survivals from a prehistoric past or simply animals that have not yet been properly identified. Probably we shall never know, unless one is captured, and that, if their reported size is accurate, may be more than a little difficult!

unicorn

To most people today, the unicorn is probably best known as a rather beautiful heraldic beast. We can see it, for example, depicted in the Royal Arms of Great Britain, standing proudly on its hind legs, facing the lion, with the shield bearing the Royal Standard between them. A noble-looking animal it is, too, white

and horse-like, except for the single, spiral-shaped horn that sprouts from the centre of its forehead.

Sadly, the unicorn never existed as a living animal. The horned horse was, and is, wholly fabulous, although that did not stop people from firmly believing in it in ancient times, particularly in Europe, the Middle East and in countries like China and Japan. There were even those who claimed to have seen one or knew someone who had, though most of these early descriptions were not very similar to the handsome beast of heraldry or medieval romance. One such account said that the unicorn had the body of a horse (though some said an antelope), but a stag's or goat's head, the feet of an elephant and the tail of a lion or bear! Its horn was a yard long, coloured black, and its voice a deep lowing sound, like that of an ox. Since the Greeks and Romans said the unicorn's home was somewhere in far-off India, some have suggested that descriptions like this actually refer to occasional early sightings of the Indian rhinoceros, which does at least have one, rather short horn, whereas the African rhino has two.

*Indian rhino -
the rhinoceros unicornis.*

Rhinoceros by Durer, 1515.

If the rhinoceros *was* the original unicorn, then it is pretty clear that a lot of imagination was needed to turn it into the far more elegant creature of later myth and legend. Indeed, some say that the unicorn we 'know' today owes its origins to other animals, such as the Arabian oryx, a beautiful if rather rare antelope which was rather more common in ancient times than it is today. The oryx isn't exactly like the unicorn of myth, of course, and has two horns, but it does display features which fit popular ideas of the unicorn. One of them is its great running speed, which makes it just as difficult to approach as the unicorn was supposed to be. Even the oryx's two, slightly curved horns might often have appeared as one when viewed from the side and at a distance. At least the oryx comes rather closer to later illustrations of the unicorn than the rhinoceros does!

In Europe, by the time of the Middle Ages, the unicorn was not only believed to exist in its distinctive, horse-like form, it had been given a definite character. Stories said that it was fierce and quite unconquerable and kept to remote areas. The only person who could approach it was a gentle maiden, who was able to tame

Scimitar-horned oryx.

Oryx gazella.

the fierce unicorn and even make it lay its head in her lap! Later, the unicorn came to signify purity (indicated by its white colour), in addition to supreme courage, strength, and nobility — all of which made it a very suitable subject to display on the coats of arms of kings and nobles.

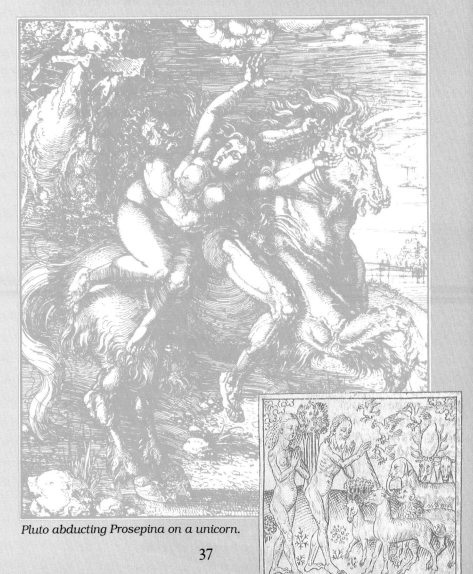

Pluto abducting Prosepina on a unicorn.

The fact that no one had ever seen a proper unicorn only served to make it more interesting and worth seeking. This was particularly so because its horn was believed to have miraculous healing powers. A cup made from a unicorn horn was supposed to protect or warn the drinker when poison was placed in it. Such reputed powers prompted kings and princes to offer high prices for any unicorn horn that came their way. After all, they could afford it and, because they were often tyrants, were the most likely to be poisoned! Not surprisingly, traders and merchants did their best to fill the demand, offering horns from all sorts of animals brought back from far-off places, and passing them off as those of the fabulous unicorn. Some were probably rhinoceros horns, while

Throne in Rosenberg Castle, Denmark. Made in 1665 for Frederick III, with pillars of unicorn horn now thought to be teeth of the sea-unicorn, the narwhal.

Narwhal.

others seem to have been those of the narwhal or 'sea unicorn', a type of whale which lives in the Arctic Ocean. The narwhal's 'horn' is really an elongated tooth, but that hardly mattered because the buyers neither knew nor cared. The point was that it really looked like the horn of the mythical unicorn: spiral-shaped and tapering almost to a point and sometimes up to one and a half metres long.

Many of these narwhal teeth ('unicorn horns') were brought by Icelandic Northmen, who were famous sailors. They caught the great beasts and, apart from using their flesh, probably did a roaring trade in their teeth, especially when, as sometimes happened, they were lucky enough to capture a narwhal with two 'horns' rather than the usual one! One of these teeth is said to have changed hands for over £10,000 when it was sold in 1598 — a great deal of money in those days.

ermaids

There is a scientific theory that man's ancestors began and evolved in the sea.

The idea is based partly on the fact that in our earliest days, in our mother's womb, we display structures which in fishes develop into gills, especially adapted for breathing water-dissolved oxygen. We lose these primitive gills later, and eventually breathe atmospheric air by means of lungs, but biologists tell us that this similarity in early development suggests that human beings and fish may have had a common marine ancestor.

Perhaps these immeasurably ancient links with the sea explain why early man was quite convinced that creatures, half-human, half-fish, lived in the world's oceans. He called them *mer-people* — mermaids and mermen — the 'mer' deriving from the Old English word for lake or sea, *mere*. Sailors, in particular, even claimed to have seen them, perhaps sitting on a rock by the seashore, combing their long yellow or sometimes sea-green hair. They were described as being human to the waist, with fish-like or dolphin-like tails below.

Such stories of mer-people occur right down the ages and in many parts of the world, especially in those countries with a maritime tradition of fishing and seafaring. They can be found in both traditional folklore, handed down from generation to generation by word of mouth, and in fiction. We can see signs of past belief in mermaids in church carvings, as well as in many inn signs.

Japanese fake mermaid.

Actually, the mer-people were not the earliest fish-like people our ancestors believed in. Far more ancient than these were gods like the Babylonian sea-god, Oannes, who, 5000 years B.C., was believed to live beneath the waves with his equally fish-tailed wife and children. More famous still was the Greek god of the seas, Poseidon (Neptune to the Romans), who was commonly shown wearing a crown and holding a three-pointed spear or trident. Poseidon was attended by fish-tailed hand-maidens, as well as dolphins, and there were also sea-nymphs like Tritons, Nereids and Sirens. Some of

Nereid on a seabull, Rome, 100 B.C.

Oannes

these, especially the Sirens, sang sweet songs which might lure sailors to their doom. Mermaids might occasionally do the same, and there are many tales of men being lured beneath the waves by mermaids, although sometimes the reverse happened and mermaids fell in love with land-living men and left the sea for a time, sometimes forever.

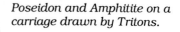

Poseidon and Amphitite on a carriage drawn by Tritons.

Gradually, as Christianity took hold in Europe, belief in half-human sea-gods declined, but the idea that the rather more human and friendly mer-people might still exist lingered on and has continued almost to the present day. Many years ago, even scientists felt that the mer-people might be living creatures and some actually went so far as to describe and illustrate them in their books. One of these, the 19th century zoologist, William Swainson, believed in them because they fitted nicely into his ideas of the relationships between animals. There ought, he felt, to be a sort of half-way stage between fish-like seals and the monkeys and apes, so what better than the mermaid! We can scarcely wonder at ordinary people firmly believing in mermaids and mermen when famous scientists confirmed their existence. In any case, it is probably true to say that people *wanted* to believe in them, just as there are those today who insist that the Loch Ness Monster and the Abominable Snowman (or 'yeti') exist, even though there is no firm evidence for either.

The Amboina mermaid 'drawn from life' in 1717.

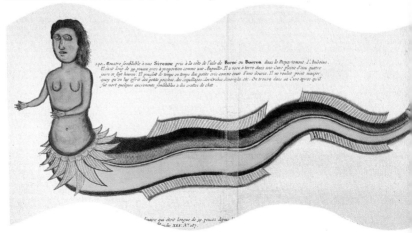

Psychologists tell us that if you believe in something strongly enough you'll quite probably 'see' it, and this seems to have been the case with those who reported sightings of mermaids. Just what they saw is not always easy to say, although various suggestions have been given. One explanation is that the 'mermaids' may have been a type of marine mammal called the sea-cow, one of which, the dugong, lives off the coasts of India and Australasia, the other, called the manatee, inhabits the water around South America and West Africa. Neither animal is very like a human being, but they do have features which might have helped people believe they were mermaids, especially when glimpsed from a distance. For one thing, they have vaguely human-like faces, while the females possess large teats, not unlike human breasts. They also tend to congregate in groups and stand near the shore, half out of the water, resting on their flippers and hind-parts. Occasionally, the females

Manatees.

cradle a pup in their fore-flippers, just as the mermaid of legend was supposed to hold her baby. If you already firmly believed in mermaids, then, it would not have taken much imagination to turn a dugong or manatee into a mermaid. When Christopher Columbus saw a group of manatees off the coast of Haiti in 1493 he immediately took them for mermaids, but expressed disappointment because they were by no means as beautiful as he had been led to believe!

Christopher Columbus lands in America

Neptune with nymphs and sea-creatures, 4th century A.D.

Of course, sea-cows — dugongs and manatees — could not be the direct origin of *all* the mermaid tales, because they do not live around the coasts of Northern Europe, where many believed in mermaids. Reports of them, brought back from distant parts, merely strengthened people's ideas of their existence. One interesting point is that even science seems to suggest that the sea-cows might provide the basis for many mermaid tales because the animals' scientific name is *Sirenia*, after those mythical Sirens, or sea-nymphs, who had beautiful voices. Sadly, the link falls rather flat because the living *Sirenia* can do no more than grunt! Other sea mammals, such as seals, have a rather better voice and indeed their cries can sometimes sound remarkably human, so it is not unlikely that people often fancied they came from mermaids, especially if heard at night when the imagination tends to run more wildly.

People were not content to see mermaids at a distance, or hear them, either. They even insisted they had caught them in their fishing nets or found them washed up on the seashore. Some of these finds are impossible to explain, except in terms of superstitious fancy, but others may merely have been creatures which the catchers (firmly believing in mermaids, remember!) had never seen before. Some were probably half decomposed remains of dolphins, porpoises, or seals, or perhaps large and unusual fish, like the weird monkfish and sea-bishop, which are sometimes very large (up to two metres long) with ugly, vaguely human-like shapes.

Interest in mermaids was often so great in the past that unscrupulous people even went so far as to forge them, for exhibition at fairs. Clearly, it would not have been easy to get away with living 'mermaids' (people wearing fish-like tails), but dead ones were a different matter. Some such fakes were cleverly made of parts of different animals carefully joined together: perhaps the head, trunk and arms of a monkey and the tail of a large fish, porpoise, or dolphin. Occasionally, these mermaids sold for large sums of money, and some even deceived scientists, especially since their owners were not willing to allow close examination. Nowadays, of course, we have no such problems, not merely because we do not believe in mermaids but because x-rays would reveal the deception straight away!

Drawing of a mermaid-fake exhibited by P.T. Barnum in the 1870s.

 giants

If we want to describe something as being exceptionally large or impressive — let us say, a building or an explosion — we might use the word 'titanic'. *Titanic* was also the name of a famous ship, then the largest ever built, which sank after colliding with an iceberg in 1912.

The word actually comes from the Titans, who were the giant sons of the Greek god Uranus (whose name, in turn, is now given to one of the planets of our solar system). Uranus had other huge sons, called the Cyclops, whose main distinction was that they each had only one eye, set in the middle of their foreheads. Another famous giant of myth was Atlas, who was so huge that he was supposed to hold the Earth on his immense shoulders, and has given us our modern name for a book of maps.

Atlas.

Odysseus puts out Cyclops' eye.

49

Somewhat smaller giants are described in fairy tales, as well as in many stories of romance and knightly chivalry, while probably the best-known giant of all was Goliath who, in the Bible, is mentioned as being one of the army of the Philistines. Goliath was quite puny as giants go, being described as six cubits and a span tall. (A cubit is an ancient Hebrew measure generally accepted as being about 45 centimetres, while a span was 22 centimetres, so you can work out his height for yourself!)

Obviously, most giants were purely mythical and could not possibly have existed, but there are others which make us stop and think and wonder if they might have been based on *some* sort of fact, at least. Most human beings rarely

David and Goliath.

grow taller than about 1.8 - 2 metres yet there are records of men attaining heights much greater than that. The tallest properly authenticated man ever known to have lived was an American, who was an amazing 2.71 metres tall and weighed 196 kilograms when he died in 1940 at the age of only 23.

Even taller men may have lived in the past; however, the further back we go the less reliable records become.

Robert Pershing Wadlow, the tallest man of all time, being measured for a suit.

In 1792 a huge thigh-bone or femur, 81 centimetres long, was found in the reputed grave of Little John, the friend of the famous outlaw, Robin Hood, in the church yard at Hathersage in Derbyshire. Where the bone went no one seems to know, but if it was authentic it ought to have made its original owner between 2.75 and 3 metres tall! The point is, though, that we cannot now be sure whether the bone was really human or not. (Strangely enough, by the way, there are very few records of giant women.)

In stories, of course, human giants are almost invariably described as immensely strong, just like the vastly bigger ones of myth and legend. Unfortunately, this is where fiction departs from fact, because from what we know about real giant men — those over about 2.10 metres — they rarely combine strength with their greater height. What such people gain in height, they lose in physical and mental power. They also generally die young (like our tall American), rarely living beyond the age of about forty. This is because exceptionally tall men nearly always suffer from certain physical defects, brought about by over-activity of a gland, at the base of the brain, called the pituitary gland. This causes an increase in height but also makes the bones uneven in size and strength. In addition, it is often accompanied by poor eyesight (even blindness) and inferior intelligence.

Giant by Doré.

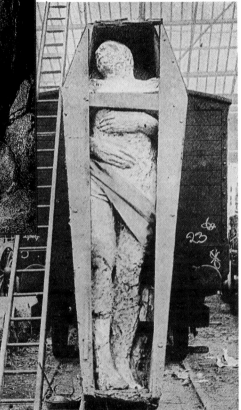

Fossilized Irish giant left at Broad Street station, London, in 1876. He was 3.70 metres tall, weighed 2,775 kilograms, and had six toes on his right foot!

If we compare these points with the giants of tradition we can find both similarities and differences. The fabulous giant might have been described as being large, powerful and fierce, but he was often rather clumsy and poor-sighted (like the one-eyed Cyclops!). He was also, more often than not, much less clever than his human opponents and therefore easily outwitted.

Orang utan.

Gorilla.

It may not have been just unusually tall or strange men that inspired the stories of giants, either. When the great gorilla of Central Africa was first seen by western man in the early 1600s he was described as being like a huge, hairy man, and all kinds of terrible tales were told about him. He was said, quite wrongly of course, to attack at every opportunity and even to carry off women and children. In Borneo and Sumatra, the orang-utan, another kind of ape, was once half-believed to be a strange human being and was, in fact, long referred to as the 'wild man of Borneo'. (Orang-utan is itself Malay for 'wild man of the woods'.)

Nowadays, we know the gorilla and the orang-utan to be no more than distant relatives of man, yet there are still those who believe in the existence of semi-human creatures, like the yeti, or 'abominable snowman', of Tibet and the Sasquatch, or 'bigfoot', of North America. Occasionally, these strange beings are described as being up to 2.75 metres tall, which puts them well into the 'giant' category! It is doubtful if they really exist, however, and even if they do they are unlikely to be human but more probably some strange animal.

Bigfoot, filmed by Roger Patterson at Bluff Creek, Northern California, 1967.